I0606507

ULTIMATE

STREET MAGIC

ULTIMATE

STREET MAGIC

Amazing tricks for the urban magician

Gary Sumpter

San Diego Public Library
Logan   DEC 1 1 2011

3 1336 07664 976

NEW HOLLAND

First published in 2006 by New Holland Publishers (UK) Ltd
London • Cape Town • Sydney • Auckland
www.newhollandpublishers.com

Garfield House, 86–88 Edgware Road,
London W2 2EA, United Kingdom

80 McKenzie Street, Cape Town 8001,
South Africa

14 Aquatic Drive, Frenchs Forest,
NSW 2086, Australia

218 Lake Road, Northcote, Auckland,
New Zealand

Copyright © 2006 in text: Gary Sumpter
Copyright © 2006 in photographs: Duncan Soar
Copyright © 2006 New Holland Publishers (UK) Ltd

10 9 8 7 6 5 4 3 2 1

All rights reserved. No part of this publication may be reproduced,
stored in any retrieval system or transmitted, in any form or by
any means, electronic, mechanical, photocopying, recording or
otherwise, without the prior written permission of the publishers
and copyright holders.

ISBN 1 84537 307 3

Publishing Manager: Jo Hemmings
Project Editor: Gareth Jones
Editor: Sarah Larter
Photography Direction & Design: Gülen Shevki-Taylor
Photographer: Duncan Soar
Index: Cathy Heath
Production: Joan Woodroffe

Reproduction by Modern Age Repro House Ltd, Hong Kong
Printed & bound in Malaysia by Times Offset (M) Sdn Bhd

DISCLAIMER: Although the author and publishers have made every
effort to ensure that the information in this book was accurate at
the time of going to press, they accept no responsibility for any
accident, loss or inconvenience sustained by any person using this
book or the advice given in it. Children practising and performing
the tricks in this book should be supervised by an adult.

contents

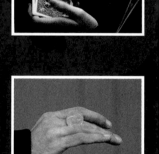

Built into the mind is an inherent desire to be mystified and amazed, so humans have long been fascinated by magic. Throughout history, magic has taken many different guises and it has evolved into an art form that spans all languages, cultures and ages.

The first magic was very simple, both in method and presentation. The earliest known magic tricks originated in the 14th century with the creation of the cups and balls effect, which is still performed by many professional magicians today. This effect gave birth to magic as a performance art and was the first step of the ladder that we stand on today.

Looking back through history, magic has typically been a stage or cabaret performance, reserved for those that were fortunate enough to visit the glossy establishments it was performed in. Today, magic is more popular and accessible than it has ever been.

It has been forced to evolve in order to keep up with the demand for ever more amazing, more impossible magic. Today, it is a much more communal art form that can be enjoyed by anybody.

Over the past few years, we have witnessed the birth of a new type of magic. No longer must we watch magicians in sweeping tailcoats and top hats, no more must we eagerly anticipate the rabbit being pulled from the hat. This new development has been cunningly titled 'Street Magic'. Performers can be found all over the world practising it. Wherever you go - pubs, clubs, markets and restaurants - you may see someone entertaining the crowds with their magical offerings.

Street Magic has become immensely popular, particularly with the introduction of televised street magicians, such as David Blaine and Paul Zenon, and quite rightly so! These performers have shown us

how effective magic can be when it is performed up close and (very) personal. Although seeing this kind of magic on television imbues it with a real air of excitement - seeing it performed live is something that you will not forget!

For as long as I can remember I have been passionate about magical performance. It started at a very early age with the celebrity magicians that appeared on our screens. I grew up watching performers like Paul Daniels, Wayne Dobson and Fred Kapps and developed huge respect for them.

As I have grown up, magic has grown, probably faster that I have! Although I still love the old ways, I am captivated by the new wave of magic. I love being able to perform for friends and associates during the course of my busy lifestyle. Having knowledge of effects that can be performed at a moment's notice is an invaluable tool. These 'tricks' can earn you friends, lovers, business and drinks - and sometimes all four!

Within the pages of this book I will share with you some top quality effects that you can use to wow anyone who cares to watch and, trust me, they will watch! Each chapter of this book concentrates on one area of magic and will offer you a range of effects.

All of the effects included in this book are relatively easy to perform, leaving you plenty of room to work on your performance. All you will need to perform the techniques described are everyday objects that are readily available.

I hope you enjoy this book and have as much fun performing magic as I do.

Best in magic
Gary Sumpter

streetcard

Card magic never fails to impress onlookers.
The next time that you have a deck of cards
handy, try one of the tricks that follow and
watch the crowds gather around you.

Snatch

TRICK: You take two cards from a deck and show them to your spectators. You then place the cards into two separate places in the deck. With a flick, you toss the deck from one hand to the other, and reveal that you have 'snatched' the two cards back from the middle of the deck!

REQUIREMENTS: A deck of cards.

1. Remove the following cards from the deck: the Nine of Hearts; the Seven of Clubs; the Seven of Hearts and the Nine of Clubs.

2. Place the Nine of Hearts on the bottom of the face-down deck of cards.

3. Now place the Seven of Clubs on top of the deck with the the Seven of Hearts and the Nine of Clubs above it. You are now ready to begin.

3. Take the top two cards from the deck - the Seven of Hearts and the Nine of Clubs. Casually show them to your audience. Be careful not to draw too much attention to the cards - allow your spectators only a brief glimpse.

TIP: This trick is best performed one-on-one, and also not for your most observant spectator, as they may notice the discrepancy! Don't rush the trick, but don't hang about either...

Snatch

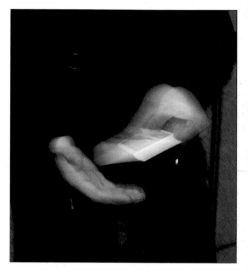

4. Turning the two cards face down, insert each one into a different part of the deck. Square the deck up so that the two cards appear to be completely lost.

5. Toss the deck of cards from one hand to the other, gripping the deck with your thumb at the top and fingers on the bottom, as shown here.

6. As the deck moves from one hand to the other, your fingers should prevent the bottom card from moving and your thumb should hold on to the top card.

7. If you toss the deck over quickly, your spectator will not realize that you took the top and bottom card. Instead, it will look like you have snatched two cards from the deck.

8. Turn over the cards in your hand: the Nine of Hearts and the Seven of Clubs. Because the cards that you lost in the deck are so close in appearance to the cards that you 'snatched' from the deck, your spectator will be fooled into thinking that they are actually the same.

The Ambitious Nines

TRICK: You take out a deck of cards and a 'prediction' card. You ask your spectator to shuffle the deck of cards, and deal them into three piles. Your spectator then turns the three piles over to discover that the bottom card of each pile matches your prediction card!

REQUIREMENTS: A deck of cards.

1. Secretly remove the four Nines from the deck. Place them into your pocket, and turn the faces inwards.

2. Bring out the deck of cards and one of the Nines from your pocket. Tell your spectator that you would like him to shuffle the cards, but before he does, you would like to make a prediction.

3. Place the Nine face down on the table, ensuring that nobody sees which card it is. Tell your spectator that this is your 'prediction' card.

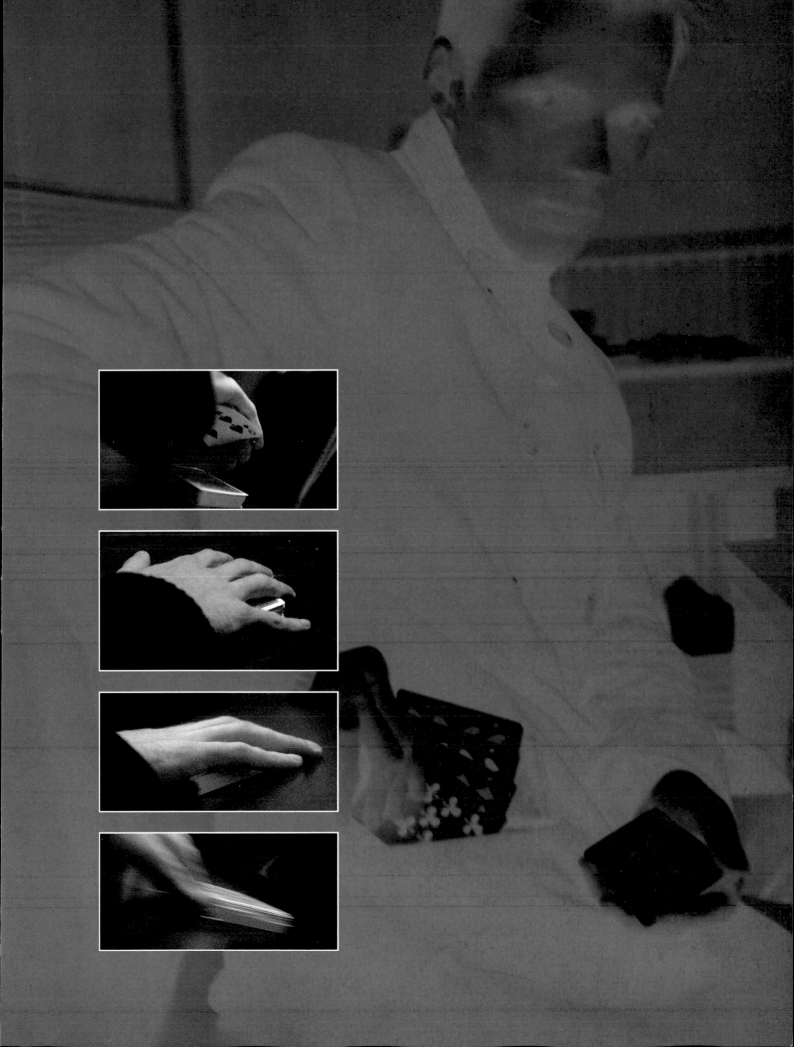

The Ambitious Nines

4. Hand the deck to your spectator and ask him to give the cards a really thorough shuffle.

5. As he is shuffling the cards, ask him to place the deck onto the table as soon as he has finished. While this is happening, casually put your hand in your pocket and bring out the remaining Nines, secretly holding them.

6. 'Palming' the three cards as shown, place your hand onto the deck (refer to the photo sequence on page 19).

7. With the three Nines safely on the top of the deck, push it towards your spectator.

8. Ask your spectator to deal the cards into three piles, one card at a time, until he has run out. Without knowing it, he will have dealt a Nine at the bottom of each apparently mixed pile.

9. Turn over your prediction card to reveal that it is a Nine.

10. Ask your spectator to turn over each of the three piles in front of him. He will be amazed to see the other three Nines!

TIP: *It is important that you get your spectator to turn over the three piles. When they think back to the trick they won't remember seeing you touch the cards.*

Restoration

TRICK: You choose a card from the deck and tear it into four pieces, one of which you give to your spectator to hold. Squeezing the other three pieces with your fingertips, you reveal that these three sections have fused back together. The missing piece exactly matches the one your spectator has been holding the whole time!

REQUIREMENTS: A deck of cards; one duplicate card; a pen.

1. Take the duplicate card and fold it into quarters. Unfolding the card, carefully tear a quarter section out of it, then fold the bigger section back into 'quarters'.

2. Pop the torn piece of card (i.e. the secret piece) into your inside pocket with the pen and place the rest of the folded card in your right hand, hidden from view. Locate the matching card from the deck and move it on to the top of the deck.

3. You now need to force this top card on to your spectator. Hold the deck face-up (the force card is now on the bottom). Using the fingers of your other hand, pull off a few cards at a time from the top of the deck, allowing them to fall into your hand – this will look like you are shuffling the cards. Ask your spectator to say stop at any point. When they do, simply stop, turn over the remaining cards and push off the top face-down card. This is, of course, the force card, but they will assume that it is a random card from the middle of the deck.

TIP: *The real key to the success of this trick is convincing your spectator that they have a completely free choice of any card.*

Restoration

4. Surreptitiously bring out the secret piece with your right hand. Holding it so it is hidden from view, fold the forced card into quarters in the same way you did in Step 1.

5. With the secret card quarter still hidden from view, slowly tear along the creases created, ripping the card into four 'quarter' pieces.

6. Show your audience the four pieces, then square them up, loading the secret piece onto the bottom of the pile. To your spectators, it still seems that you have a pile of four pieces of card - in reality there are now five.

7. Flip the pile over. The secret piece is now at the top of the pile. Tell your spectator that you want to give them a little souvenir of your performance. Take off the top piece of card (the secret piece) and hand it to them. You now have all four pieces of the spectator's card.

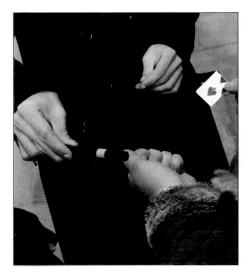

8. Tell your spectator that you, like all magicians, need a magic wand to help you, but as you don't have one, you will use a pen. Reach into your inside pocket with your right hand to grab the pen. As your hand goes into your pocket, drop the pieces of card that you are holding and pick up the extra card that you previously placed in there. Also pick up the pen. You must do this very quickly, so as not to arouse any suspicion.

9. Transfer the card into your free hand, spreading it slightly, to create the illusion that it is still in three separate pieces. Place the 'pile' into your spectator's palm and ask them to close their hand into a tight fist.

10. Wave the pen over their fist in your most theatrical way, and then ask them to open their hand.

11. Slowly open up the card to show that the three pieces have, apparently, fused back together. You can now place the spectator's piece in the gap to show that it does indeed match perfectly.

The Dextrous Disappearance

TRICK: You take a borrowed card and make it disappear into thin air.

REQUIREMENTS: One playing card.

1. Hold the card at your fingertips, with your thumb in front and your fingers behind.

2. Holding the card in place with your thumb, move your index and little fingers outwards, gripping the card at its long edges. As you do this, bend your middle fingers at the knuckle behind the card.

3. With your index and little fingers still gripping the card, move your thumb out of the way, and extend your middle and ring fingers. This will pivot the card behind your hand.

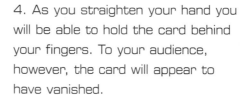

4. As you straighten your hand you will be able to hold the card behind your fingers. To your audience, however, the card will appear to have vanished.

TIP: To make this seem even more convincing, give the card a tossing motion, as though you are throwing it up into the air. It will take some practice to combine this motion with the flipping of the card, but it is well worth it! (See the photo sequence opposite for guidance.)

streethustler

People love money — watching it, playing with it and spending it! Performing magic tricks with somebody else's hard-earned cash will send your audience head-over-tails with amazement!

Kangaroo

TRICK: You borrow two coins from a spectator and place one on the palm of each hand. Flipping your hands over, one of the coins jumps from one hand to the other.

REQUIREMENTS: Two borrowed coins.

1. Hold the borrowed coins out, one in each palm. Note the position shown here - the coin in your right hand must be close to your thumb.

2. Flip your hands palm downwards.

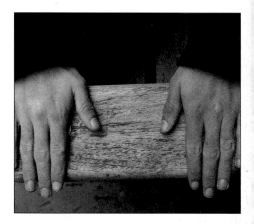

To your spectators, it will appear that there is a coin under each hand. In fact, the action of flipping your hands will throw the coin from your right hand under your left.

3. Turn your hands over to reveal that one coin has mysteriously kangarooed into the other.

TIP: *This sounds far too easy to work, but it does. With practice, the coin will automatically move over to the other hand, propelled by the action of quickly flipping your palms downwards.*

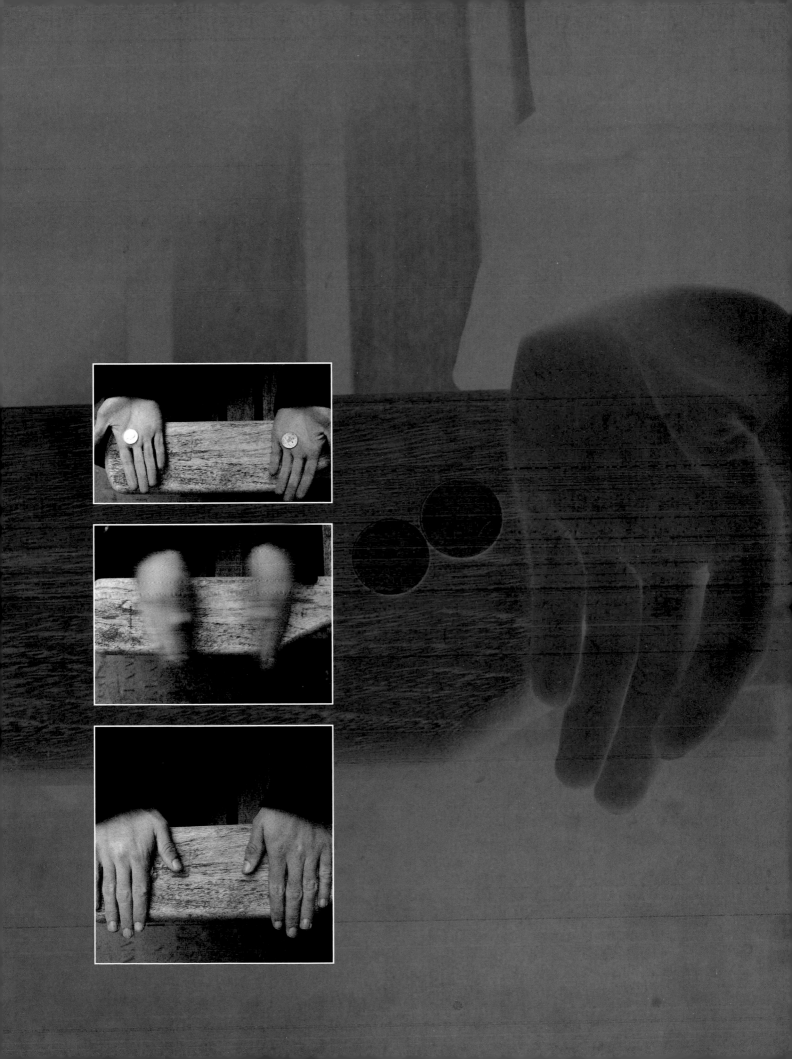

The Cost of Living

TRICK: You borrow a banknote from a spectator, fold it into a small parcel and hold it at your fingertips. Snapping your fingers, you unfold the parcel to show that it has changed into a note of lower value. That's inflation for you... When your spectator complains, you change it back to the high-value note.

REQUIREMENTS: A low-value note; a borrowed high-value note.

1. Take your low-value note and fold it in half from the left edge to the right edge. Fold it in half again from the top edge to the bottom edge. Finally fold it in half again from the left edge to the right edge and conceal it in one hand (see the full photo sequence opposite for reference).

2. Borrow a high-value banknote from a willing onlooker. Take the note from them with your free hand, then open it out with the finger and thumb of both hands.

3. Slowly fold the borrowed high-value note in half twice, as you did for the low-value note in Step 1.

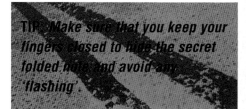
TIP: Make sure that you keep your fingers closed to hide the secret folded note and avoid any 'flashing'.

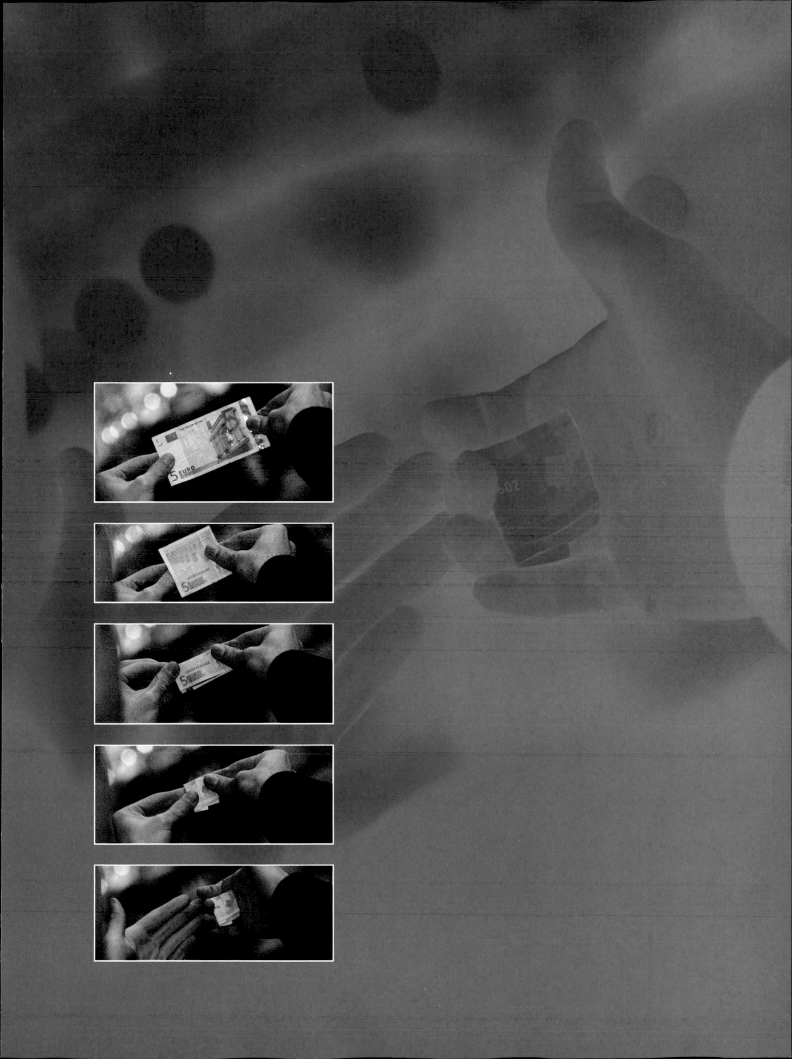

The Cost of Living

3. As you make the third fold, move the palmed low-value note to the back of the borrowed high-value note as shown.

4. When you make the final fold, turn the whole packet over. The palmed low-value banknote should now be at the front, and the onlooker's high-value note at the back.

5. Unfold the banknote from the front. This will open up the low-value note. While doing this, ensure that the high-value note remains folded behind it.

6. You can now display the low-value note in the same way as before, ensuring the folded note is hidden from view.

7. To reverse the process, do exactly the same as in the previous steps, folding the low-value note up, switching it with the one of higher value and revealing the change.

You can now return the borrowed high-value note. As you do, casually place your hand into your pocket, dropping off the low-value note and ditching the evidence!

Bank Transfer

TRICK: You borrow two differently coloured coins. Your spectator holds one coin tightly in their hand. You take the second coin, showing it to your audience and holding it at your fingertips. You rub the coin and it changes into the first coin. When the spectator opens their hand, they find the second coin inside!

REQUIREMENTS: A copper coin; two borrowed coins of a similar size – one copper, one silver – the copper coin matching your own.

1. Conceal the first copper coin in the hollow at the base of your fingers, where you should hold it securely. This is what magicians refer to as the 'finger palm'.

2. Borrow a copper coin and a silver coin from your spectator (ensuring that the copper coin matches the one you have concealed). Display the borrowed coins in the fingertips of each hand (the silver coin in the fingers of the hand hiding the first copper coin – see the photographs opposite).

3. Tell your spectator that you are going to put the silver coin into her hand. As you move your hand over her palm, turn the silver coin inwards and allow the secret copper coin to drop into its place. The silver coin should now be hidden in the 'finger palm'.

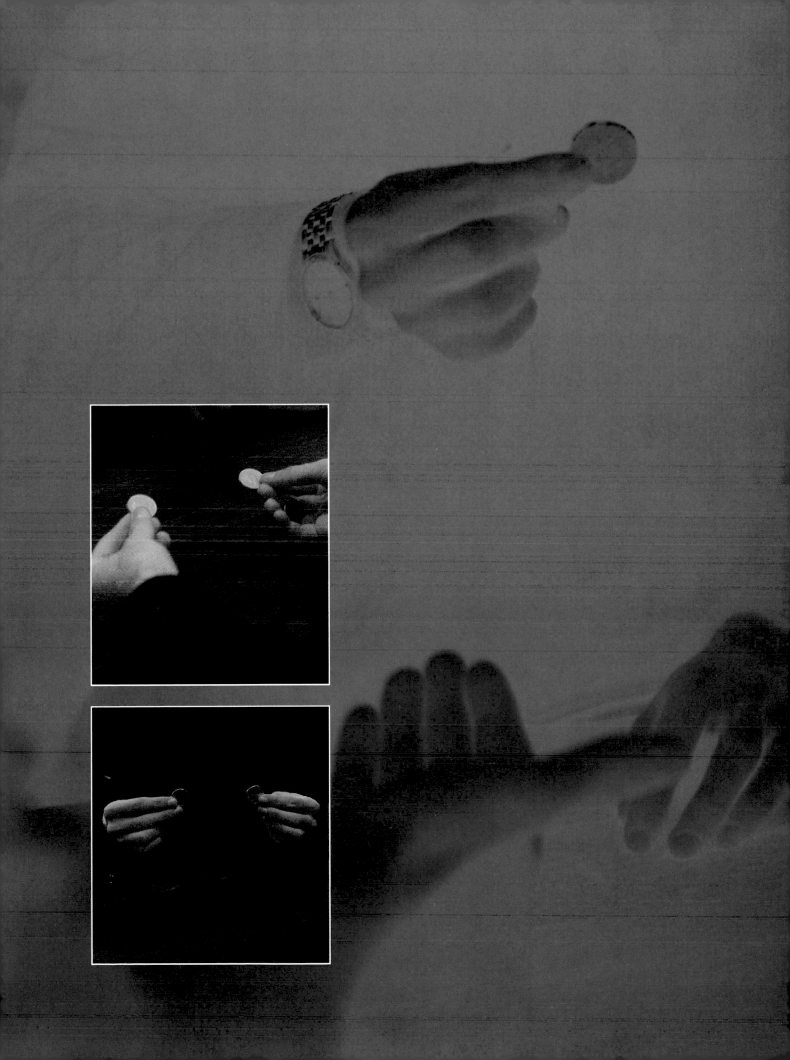

·Bank Transfer

4. As you place the copper coin onto your spectator's palm, and move the silver coin into the magician's palm position, close your spectator's hand into a fist and tell her to keep it tightly clenched. If this is all done smoothly, she will not suspect anything - she will see the silver coin move towards her hand and think she feels it land in her hand.

5. Now divert your spectator's attention to the copper coin, casually displaying it on both sides, ensuring that the silver coin remains hidden from view.

TIP: *Try this in front of a mirror. To an onlooker this trick appears to be a very clear transformation of one coin to another. The colour difference between a copper coin and a silver coin plays a big part here. This effect is well worth the practice required, as, once you have mastered the technique, you will have a real gem to amaze people for years to come!*

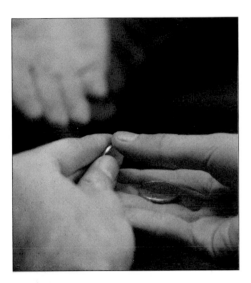

7. Bring your right hand up to the copper coin as shown and rub it a few times, as if you are trying to impart some kind of magic to the coin.

8. Gradually cover the copper coin with your fingers. Giving the copper coin a final rub, knock it back into the palm of your left hand with your thumb. As you do this, move the silver coin to the fingertips of your right hand.

9. All this is left is to ask the spectator to open their hand, revealing that the two coins really have changed places.

Squeezed and Gone

TRICK: You borrow a coin and place it on the table you are sitting at, rolling up your sleeves to dispel any suggestion of funny business. Picking the coin up with your fingertips you give it a little blow, and the coin mysteriously vanishes!

REQUIREMENTS: Any borrowed coin.

1. Begin by borrowing a coin from an onlooker, the larger the better. Place the coin on the table in front of you so that everybody can see it clearly.

2. Place your fingertips over the coin on the table, slowly drawing it towards you.

3. When the coin reaches the edge of the table, it will drop into your other hand. However, you must continue moving your fingers off the edge of the table and upwards as if the coin is still held at your fingertips. You should not pause or hesitate at this moment - smoothness is the key to making the illusion work. (See the photo sequence opposite.)

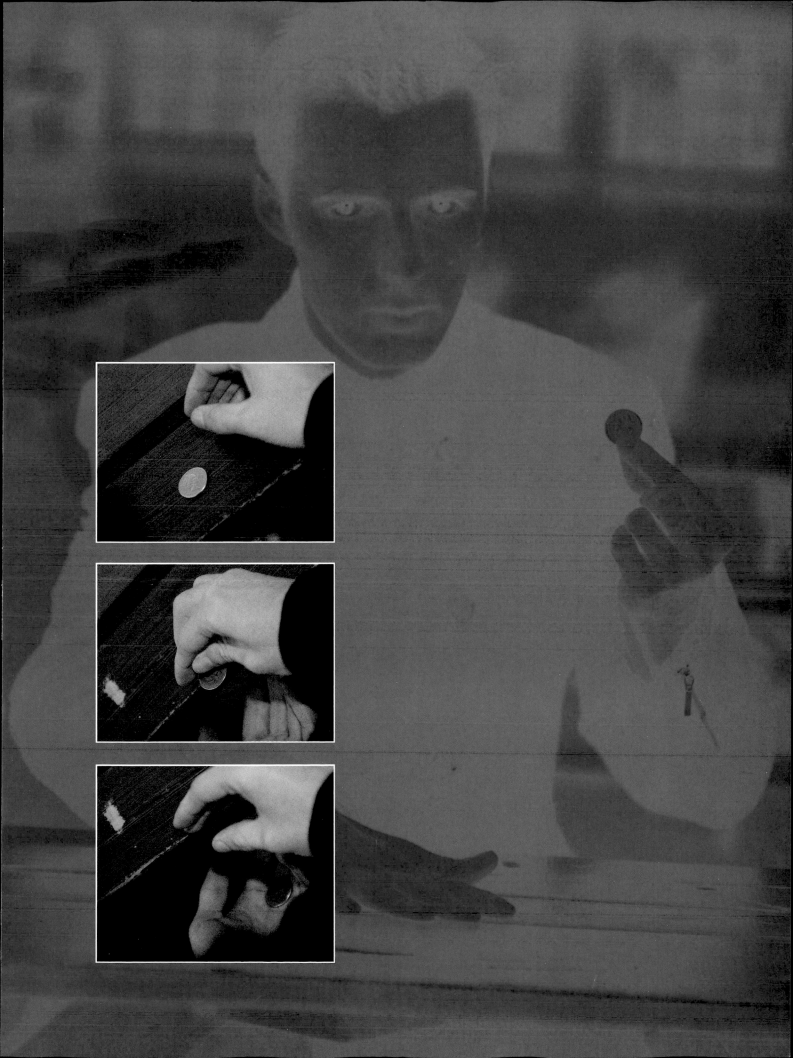

Squeezed and Gone

4. Bring your hand up as if it is still holding the coin and blow gently on your fingers.

5. Now show your audience that the coin has vanished. (Remember to pick up the coin in your lap when nobody is looking!)

6. If this is not enough to impress your audience, you can use the same moves to make it look as though the coin has melted through the table. As before, move the coin to the edge of the table with your fingertips, pretending to hold it but allowing it to drop into the palm of your other hand.

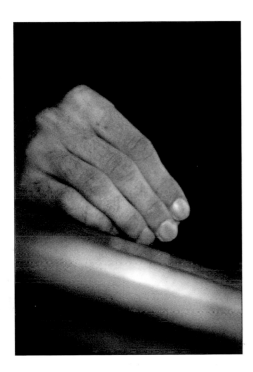

7. Tap your fingers above the table as if they contain the coin, while tapping the real coin under the table at exactly the same time. This will create the illusion that the coin is still held above the table.

8. Slap your hand onto the table and do the same underneath the table simultaneously. Again, this will sound as though you have slapped the coin onto the top of the table.

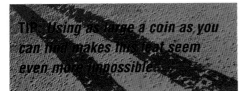

TIP: Using as large a coin as you can find makes this feat seem even more impossible.

9. Slowly lift your hand to show that the coin is no longer on the table and bring out your other hand, showing that the coin has amazingly melted through the table!

The Jumping Band

TRICK: You stretch a rubber band around your index and middle fingers. In a flash, the band jumps across to your ring and little fingers.

REQUIREMENTS: A small coloured rubber band.

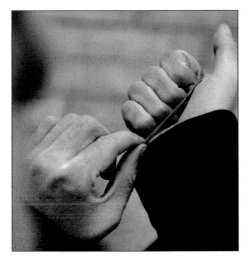

1. Begin by placing the rubber band over your index and middle fingers.

2. Now curl all four fingers inwards to make a fist, as you do so, place them inside the rubber band. (See the full photo sequence opposite left - top to bottom).

3. Hold your fist so that the rubber band appears to be looped around your index and middle fingers.

TIP: This is a basic effect that can be hyped up into a full scale Las Vegas-style illusion! Try using two bands, one on each hand and performing the technique so that both bands jump at the same time. You can also try reversing the motion, causing the bands to jump onto your index and middle fingers.

4. When you open your hand in front of your spectators, the rubber band will automatically jump onto your other two fingers. (See the full photo sequence opposite right - top to bottom).

streetband

The great thing about rubber bands is that they're cheap, visual and easy to find. These tricks are great for when your audience needs a bit of visual stimulation — they work well on their own, but they can also be stretched together into a longer routine.

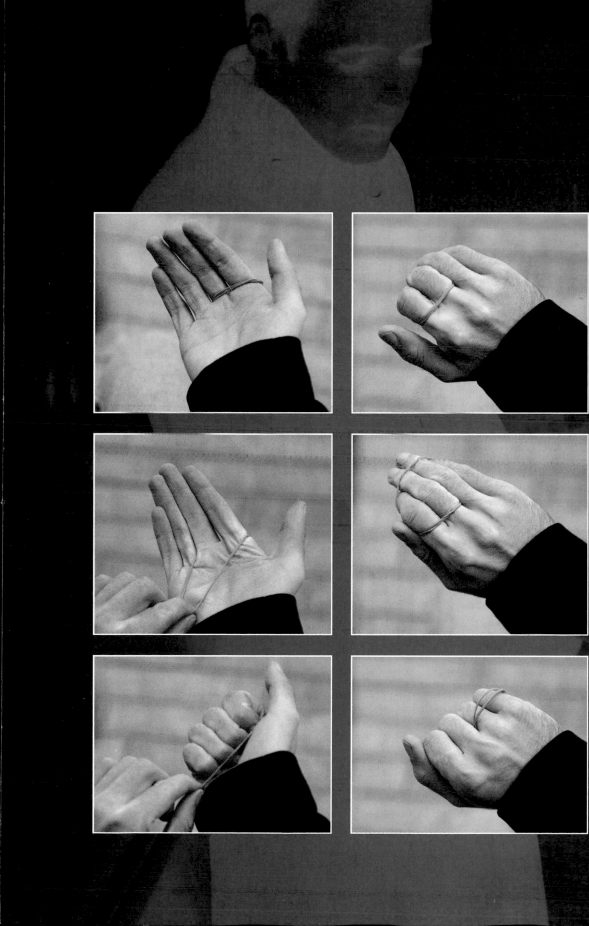

The Homing Band

TRICK: Wrapping a rubber band around your fingers, you point to the other side of the room. You shoot the rubber band off your fingers and yell, 'Come back!' The rubber band immediately comes rolling back to you!

REQUIREMENTS: A thick rubber band; plenty of floor space.

1. Take the rubber band and loop one end around your little finger. Bring it back behind your thumb and hook it over the tip of your index finger.

2. Clench your hand to stretch the band, then release with your index finger. The band should flick off your little finger towards the floor with a backward spin.

3. With practice, you can shoot the band forwards with enough backspin to cause the band to return to you immediately (see the photo sequence opposite). When mastered, this is guaranteed to impress!

TIP: When practising this trick, it is best to start with a thicker rubber band that won't slip off your fingers easily. You can then move on to thinner bands as you master the technique.

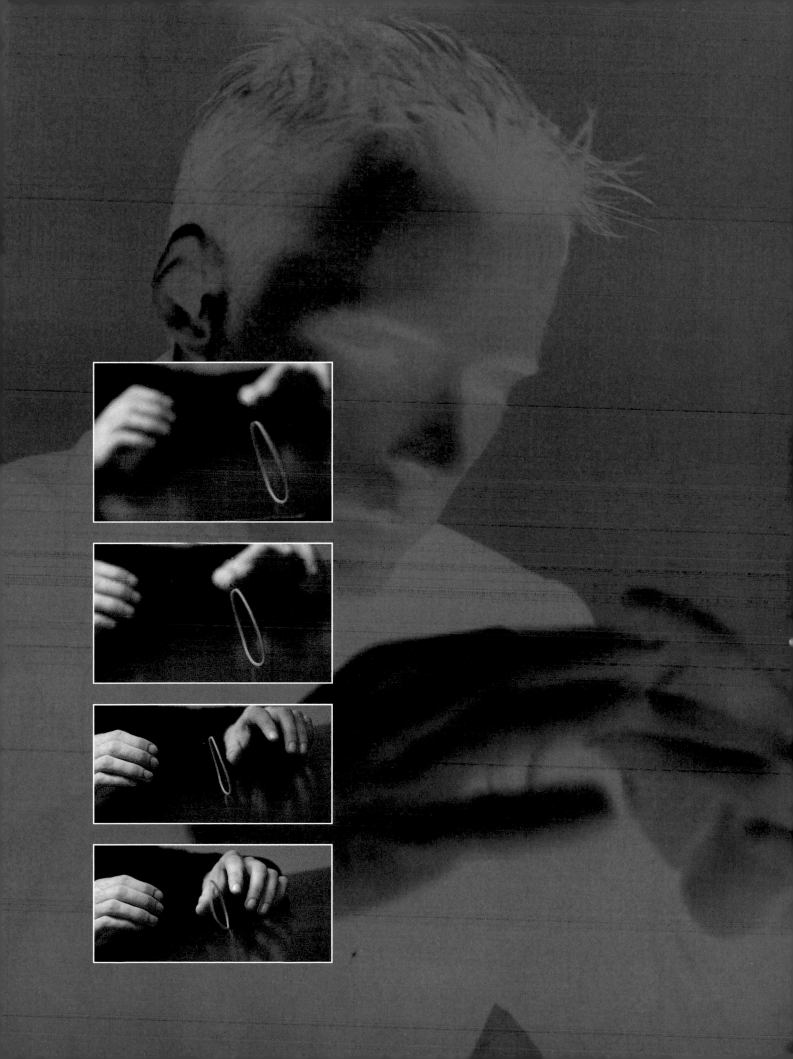

Two-to-one

TRICK: You display what looks like two rubber bands to your audience. Rubbing them together they appear to melt, leaving you with one long rubber band!

REQUIREMENTS: One thin stretchy rubber band.

1. Take the rubber band and twist it once, placing your thumbs and index fingers into the loops, as shown. which will allow you to hold it in a figure-of-eight position.

2. Move your hands apart slightly. By opening and closing your fingers alternately, you create the illusion that you have two separate bands. See the photo sequence opposite.

3. Slip the 'bands' off your fingers and rub the tangle of elastic together.

4. When you open the 'bands', they will appear to have melted together into a single rubber band.

TIP: This tricks works well when performed before 'The Jumping Band'.

50

streetfire

From the time of mankind's earliest settlements
and civilisations, people have always been both
scared and fascinated by fire — so why not harness
this deep-seated power in your magic?

Match Revival

TRICK: You light a few matches, burning them for a few seconds before dropping them into an ashtray. You then pick up one of the spent matches, concentrate for a moment and re-strike the match, causing is to burst back into life.

REQUIREMENTS: A box of matches; an ashtray; a black marker pen.

1. Begin by colouring the tip and about a quarter of the length of a match, so that it looks just like a spent match. Place this match in the ashtray and you are ready to begin.

2. Strike a few matches as you talk casually to your onlookers, dropping each one into the ashtray. When you want to perform your mini-miracle, reach into the ashtray and remove the doctored match.

TIP: Try to attract your spectator's attention away from the ashtray at the start of this trick. You want them to believe that the match you 'revive' really was one of the matches that they saw burning!

3. Strike the match against the box and it will light, as you would expect a fresh one to. It's not exactly earth-shattering, but it's definitely something to get your audience thinking!

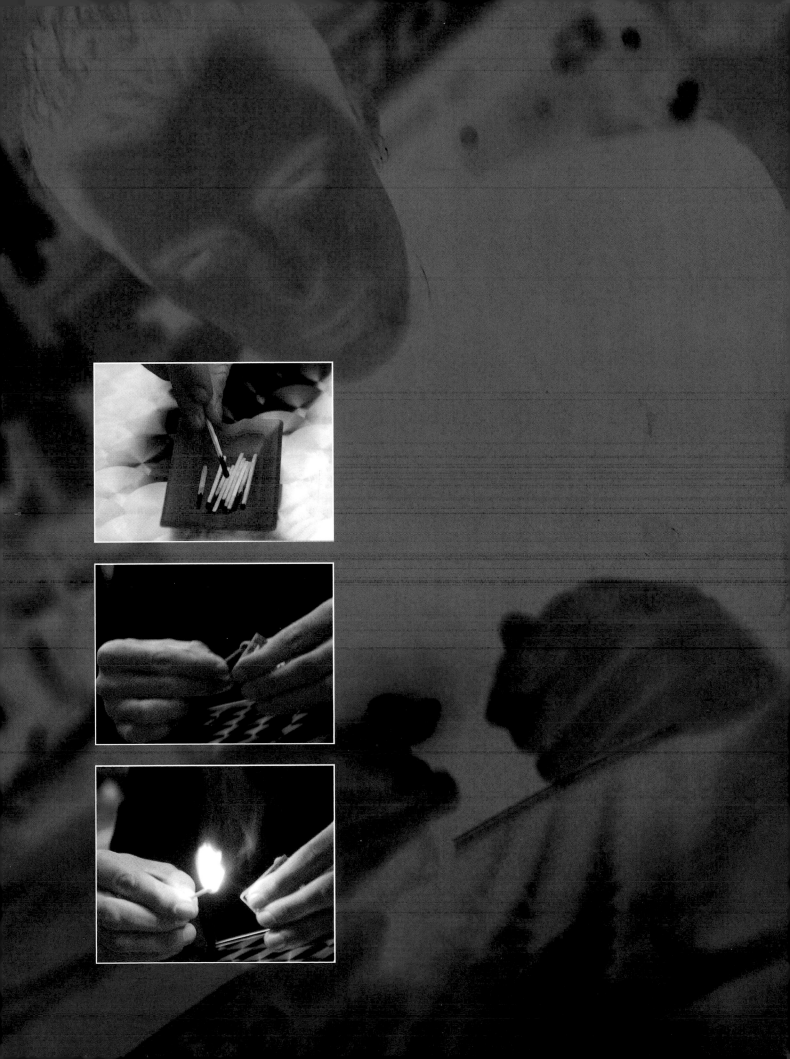

Finger Flash

TRICK: Holding a match at the fingertips of your left hand, you rub the tip between your right index finger and thumb. Almost instantly, the match mysteriously lights!

REQUIREMENTS: A box of matches.

1. We all know how to light a match - you strike it along the brown strip on the side of the matchbox. So, if you tear off one-third of the strip and fold it in half, it is a perfect size to conceal between your index finger and thumb (see the close up shots opposite).

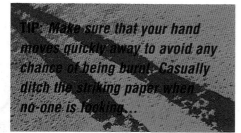

TIP: Make sure that your hand moves quickly away to avoid any chance of being burnt. Casually ditch the striking paper when no-one is looking...

2. Take a match from the box and place the tip between your right index finger and thumb.

3. Quickly pull your right hand away from the match while squeezing. The friction lights the match and means that your hand is further away from the flame!

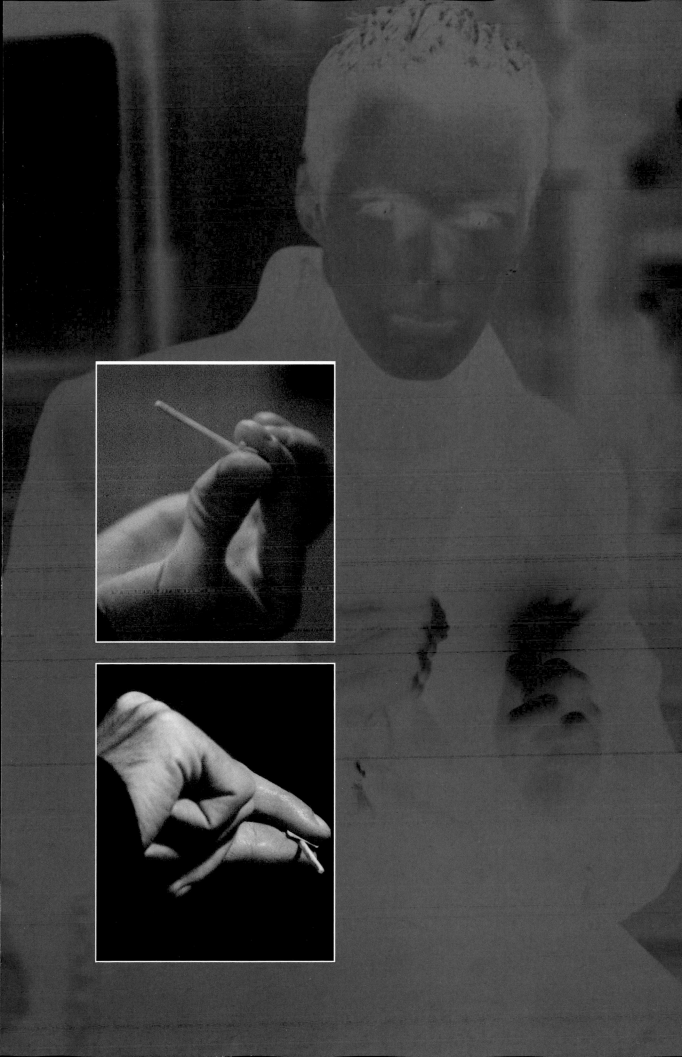

Scorcher

TRICK: A volunteer selects a card, which is put back into the deck. You then borrow a lighter and hold it under the deck for a few seconds. You spread the cards to reveal one card with a large burn mark on the back. This is your volunteer's chosen card!

REQUIREMENTS: A deck of cards; one duplicate card; a lighter.

1. Remove your chosen card from the deck. Take the duplicate card and put a large scorch mark on the back of it with the lighter. Place the scorched card on the bottom of the deck, the clean card beneath it.

2. For this trick, you will need to perform what is known as a 'Cross-cut Force'. To achieve this, ask your onlooker to split a deck of cards about halfway down, placing the pile they've taken (A) next to what is left of the original deck of cards (B).

TIP: The Cross-cut is ideal for a wide range of tricks, as it gives you complete control over which card is chosen. See the photo sequence opposite, Restoration (page 22) and Ashes (page 62) for other examples.

Scorcher

3. Pick up the remaining deck (B) and place it across the onlooker's chosen pile (A). Inform them that you're marking the point at which the cards were cut. At this stage, distract both volunteer and audience with a little banter or a few questions. This will take their minds off the trick.

4. Take the upper pile of cards (B) and flip it face up, displaying their chosen card - the one you placed on the bottom of the deck at the start. Place this pile of cards on to the other, then square the deck up.

5. Briefly wave the lighter underneath the deck for effect and then spread the cards out into a fan to reveal that one of the cards has been scorched.

6. Spread the remaining cards face-down to show that they are all normal. Turn the scorched card over to reveal that it is the same one chosen by your spectator!

Ashes

TRICK: Your volunteer chooses a playing card from the deck and writes the name of the card on a piece of paper, which you set alight. Pulling up your sleeve, you pick up a clump of the ashes from the burnt paper. You rub the ashes onto your arm and, as they fade, the name of the playing card appears.

REQUIREMENTS: A deck of cards; a piece of paper; a lighter; an ashtray; a clear lip balm; a pen.

1. To prepare, place your chosen card at the bottom of the deck. With the clear lip balm, write the number and symbol of the chosen card on your forearm. Allow the lip balm to dry and pull your sleeve down.

2. Ask your volunteer to choose a card at random from the deck. Force your chosen card on him using the Cross-cut Force (see pages 58-61 for more details) - in this case, the Two of Diamonds.

TIP: The key to making this trick work is to exaggerate the fact that you couldn't possibly have known which card was chosen.

3. Ask your volunteer to look at this card and write the name of the card on the paper with the pen.

4. Once he has done this, ask him to screw the paper up into a tight ball and drop it into the ashtray.

5. Take the lighter and set the ball of paper on fire. Now the magic can begin!

5. Pull up your sleeve to reveal that you have nothing suspicious hidden there.

6. Now take a small pile of ashes from the ashtray and slowly rub it onto your arm, over and around the lip-balmed area. Onlookers will think you are crazy, which you probably are, but stick with it.

6. At first, all that will be visible is a dark, dirty smear on your arm. Keep rubbing gently, however, and the ash will slowly disintegrate. The area around the lip balm will not have any ash left stuck to it, whereas the lip balm will absorb some of the dark colour, leaving you with pretty obvious writing on your arm... The name of your spectator's chosen card! (Refer to the photo sequence on page 63 for more detail).

streetmind

The most impressive feats of magic are those that are performed on the human mind. Use the techniques that follow to fool others into thinking that you are a modern-day mind-reader!

Three-way

TRICK: You show your volunteer a matchbox and three objects – one red, one blue and one green. You ask your volunteer to choose one of the colours, and reveal that their chosen colour had been written on the matchbox all along.

REQUIREMENTS: An empty matchbox; a pen; three coloured objects.

1. Write down the three colours as follows: red inside the tray; blue on the underside of the tray; green on the bottom of the matchbox (see the photo sequence opposite).

Show your volunteer the three coloured objects and the matchbox, ensuring you do not flash the writing on the bottom.

2. Ask your volunteer to choose one of the three colours, but to keep it secret at this stage. Here you can pretend that you are trying to influence your volunteer's decision in some clever psychological way, which, of course, you are not.

3. After a suitably dramatic pause, ask your volunteer to name their chosen colour out loud. As soon as it has been revealed, divert your audience's attention back to the matchbox. If your volunteer chose red, slide the tray out normally, to reveal 'Red', written inside. If they chose blue, turn the box upside down and slide the tray out to reveal 'Blue' on the underside (be careful to cover the writing on the bottom of the sleeve when you do this!). If they choose green simply flip the box over to reveal 'Green'.

TIP: Try to handle the matchbox as freely as possible, so as not to arouse suspicion that it may be a special matchbox. Magic with apparently 'normal' objects is always the strongest!

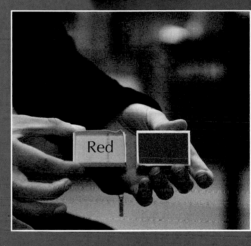

Vanishing Thought

TRICK: You offer your volunteer a fan of six playing cards and ask them to think of one, but not to name it out loud. You square up the fan and shuffle it face down, then snap your fingers and count the cards – there are only five there... You hand the cards to your volunteer and ask them to name their chosen card. When they look through the cards, it has mysteriously vanished!

REQUIREMENTS: A deck of cards.

1. Take the following cards from the deck: Ten of Clubs, King of Spades, Nine of Diamonds, Three of Hearts, Seven of Clubs and Ace of Diamonds. This is your first set.

Next, gather together the following cards: Ten of Spades, King of Clubs, Nine of Hearts, Three of Diamonds, Seven of Spades, and Ace of Hearts. This is your second set.

2. Place the first set of cards on the top of the deck, keeping them separate from the rest of the deck by sliding the tip of your little finger in between. (This is what magicians refer to as a 'break'.)

Fan the second set of cards in your right hand so that the faces are visible to your volunteer. Ask them to think of one of the cards that they see in the fan. Make sure they do not name their chosen card out loud!

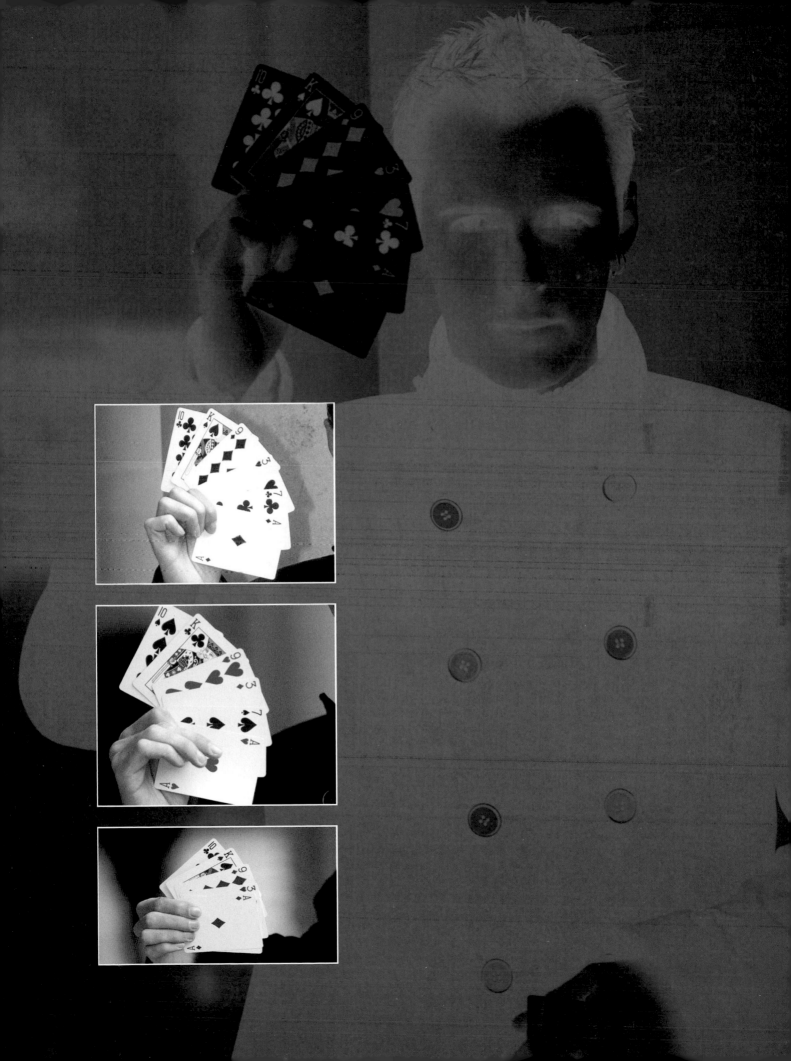

Vanishing Thought

4. When your volunteer confirms that they have selected a card from the fan (i.e. the second set), ask them to concentrate on their card. While they are doing this, drop the fan down to waist height. As you drop your right hand, bring your left hand and the deck up to meet it. (You will need to time this so that the fan covers the deck).

When the fan is directly over the top of the deck (and the first set of cards), close it, ensuring that you keep the first set separate from the rest of the deck with the tip of your little finger.

5. Now switch the second set of cards for the first set, by pushing the upper left corner of the second set into the hollow between your left thumb and index finger. You will find that the cards can be secured here, allowing you to drop your left hand to the side again, taking the deck and the second set with it, and leaving the first set behind in your right hand.

7. Ask your spectator to focus their thoughts on the card that they are thinking of. Display the set you are now holding to your them. The card they were thinking of has vanished. (In reality, as we know, every card has changed, so whichever card was in your volunteer's head will have disappeared.)

6. This whole action should be performed very swiftly, and look like you have just brought both hands together to square the cards. You should divert the spectator's attention by talking to them about the card that they are thinking of - always maintaining eye contact. Whatever happens, do not look at the move as you make it!

TIP: This effect is primarily suited for a one-to-one performance, as if two or more spectators think of different cards and they all vanish, the secret may be discovered!

Mind Over Body

TRICK: You ask your volunteer to take a seat. You press two fingers against their forehead and ask them to stand up. Amazingly, they find that they cannot – no matter how hard they try. This effect works for even the strongest person.

REQUIREMENTS: A volunteer; a chair.

1. Ask your volunteer to take a seat, telling her to sit up straight and concentrate. This is important - you want her to sit back in the chair.

Explain to your audience that the fingers are the strongest part of the human body and that, using just two of them, it is possible to overcome the strength of another person. Tell your victim that when you say the word, 'Lift', you would like her to try to stand up.

2. Placing your fingers on your volunteer's forehead, say, 'Lift.' At this point she will try to stand but won't be able to. The reason that she finds this so difficult is simply a question of balance. To understand completely, try it yourself. Sit up straight on a chair. Now stand up in the way that you normally would - the first thing you do is to lean forward! This is necessary to ensure that as you stand, you remain balanced and don't fall over! This trick works simply because you are preventing your volunteer from leaning forward.

3. Sometimes the person you ask to do the trick may try to use their arms to push themselves up. Although this is sometimes successful, it doesn't usually help, and just makes the whole business that little bit funnier!

Lift Up

TRICK: You ask a male volunteer to lift up a smaller female volunteer, which he finds fairly easy. But then, just by staring at him, you cause him to lose his strength, and he finds it almost impossible to lift the same person again.

REQUIREMENTS: A volunteer who looks strong; a second, smaller volunteer, who is in on the trick.

1. Ask your male volunteer to lift up your female volunteer. He will naturally try to lift her with his hands under her arms, and should find it fairly easy.

2. Tell him that you are now going to try to remove most of his strength so that he will find it difficult to repeat the lift. Pretend to concentrate on him, behaving as if you really are doing something.

3. Ask your male volunteer to try the lift again. This time, however, your female volunteer will place her hands just above the inside of his elbow joint. As a result he will find it virtually impossible to lift her up, because she is now at arm's length. (See the photo sequence opposite).

TIP: This trick works brilliantly with a burly guy and a small and dainty girl... Just make sure he has a sense of humour!

streetfreak

When you're a magician, people naturally expect you to be able to do weird and wonderful things... But no-one will be expecting you to perform the following tricks...

Snap

TRICK: You flex your index finger back with a sickening twist and the sound of the bone breaking! This is great to present as a warm-up for your magic routine.

REQUIREMENTS: Good acting skills!

2. With your right hand, grab your left index finger as shown. Flex the finger back a few times. When you are ready, sharply pull back the finger with your right hand, and simultaneously click your right middle finger and thumb together, in the same way you would attract a waiter's attention!

1. Tell your audience that you need to flex your fingers a little in preparation for the knuckle-busting sleight-of-hand magic that they are about to witness.

3. This snapping of the other fingers will create a loud cracking sound that is bound to turn the stomachs of anybody watching, as they will think it is the finger you are flexing!

Impaled

TRICK: You appear to thrust the prongs of a plastic fork through your finger!

REQUIREMENTS: Two plastic forks; some rubber cement. Most plastic forks come with four prongs – if yours doesn't, simply adjust accordingly.

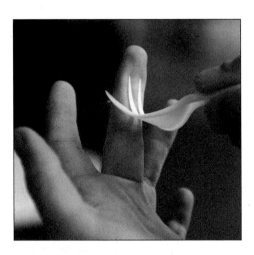

1. Remove half of the two middle prongs on one of the forks. With a little rubber cement, carefully stick them to the back of a finger at roughly the same distance apart as they were on the fork. When you are ready to cause a moment of shock, pick up your other fork. You may want to eat something with it first so that your onlookers can see it is perfectly normal.

2. When you want to 'impale' your finger, hold the fork so the prongs are pointing downwards. Push the fork against the flesh and in one swift movement, point the finger that is being impaled upwards, revealing the two half prongs that you stuck there previously.

TIP: For added effect, add a little red nail varnish to the bottom of the half prongs. When you lose the prongs at the end of the trick, you'll also leave behind a little 'scar'!

3. The two middle prongs will bend inwards and the two outer prongs will sit either side of your finger. The illusion is very quick and convincing. To finish, pull the fork away, allowing the middle prongs to return to their original shape.

As you pull the prongs out of your finger, act as if you are going to try it on someone else. Lean forward and hold the fork above their hand. As you do this, casually knock off the two half prongs from your finger.

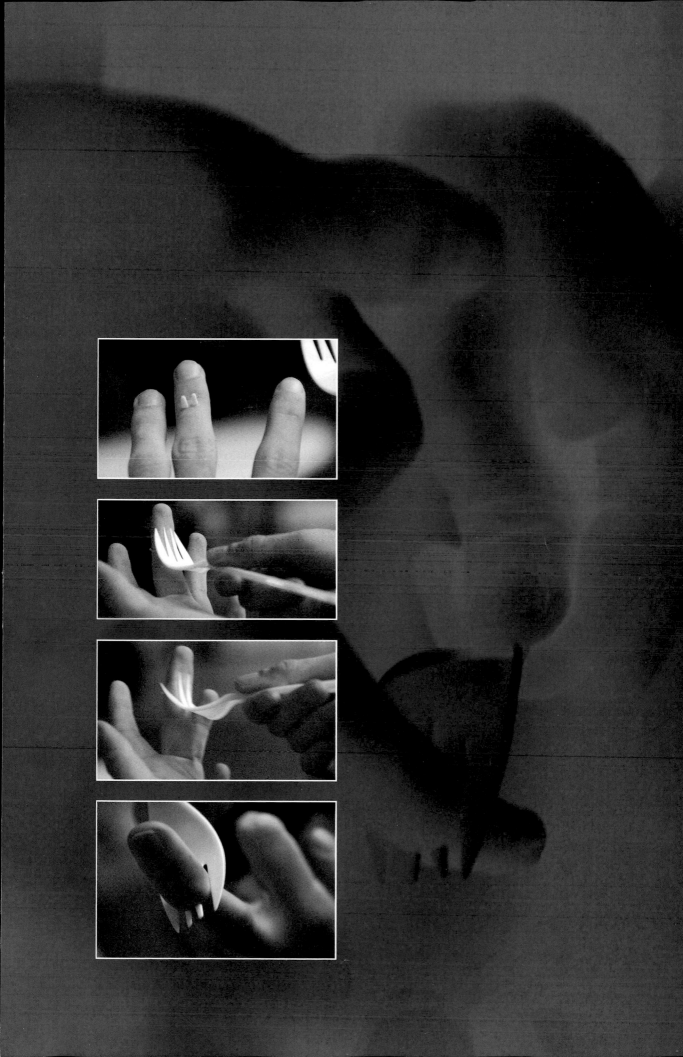

Nose-plug

TRICK: You use a small pencil to clear your sinuses, but you sniff a little too hard and it disappears up your nose!

REQUIREMENTS: Two small pencils; sticky tape.

1. Begin by taping one of the pencils to your right-hand middle finger as shown. When your right hand is open, the pencil flicks back behind the middle finger and is hidden from view. Allow this hand to hang naturally at your side.

2. With your left hand, pick up the other pencil and hold it as shown, with all your fingers curled around it.

3. Now pretend to push the pencil up your nose, while actually moving it into your left hand, behind your fingers, to create the optical illusion. Some of your onlookers may be impressed by this. Most, however, will disregard it as a funny little gag that their uncle used to do!

Nose-plug

3. Once you have apparently pushed the pencil right up your nose, drop your hand down slightly so that it is at mouth level, place the tip of the pencil into your mouth and pull, allowing the pencil to slide out of your left fingers. It looks as if you have pushed the pencil up your nose and pulled it out of your mouth. Most sensible adults, however, will not be fooled by this!

4. As you joke with your onlookers, casually drop the loose pencil below the edge of your table, into your lap.

TIP: I find that if you perform the first phase of Nose-plug as a gag, the second phase will be twice as shocking!

5. When the moment is right, bring your right hand up, as if it is holding the same pencil that was previously in the left hand.

6. Bring your left hand up, leaving the loose pencil to fall into your lap. Ensuring that your audience is on your left-hand side, open your hands as though you are about to sneeze, and then sniff sharply, opening your left hand slightly to hide the right hand. From where your audience is positioned, it looks like you have inhaled the pencil.

7. Quickly but carefully open your hands with a smooth action. The pencil is now located at the back of the fingers on your right hand.

8. With your palms out, show your audience that you are clearly not holding anything. Casually drop your right hand down when the heat is off and ditch the pencil and tape into a pocket. Don't forget to retrieve the loose pencil too!

Glassed

TRICK: You take a bottle and wrap it in a napkin or piece of cloth. You tap it a few times with a hammer until a distinct shattering sound is heard. Unfolding the material to reveal a mass of broken glass, you casually pick up a handful of glass shards and begin to eat them, crunching away and enjoying every moment. This one isn't for audience members of a nervous disposition...

REQUIREMENTS: A beer bottle; a hammer; boiled sweets that match the colour of the bottle.

1. Before you perform the trick, take a handful of the boiled sweets and smash them up roughly so you are left with a range of sizes. Place all of the broken pieces into a small pot or bag in your pocket. You are now ready to begin!

2. When you decide to perform this sick and twisted little effect, give the bottle to the onlooker to check that it's real. Offer the napkin or cloth for their inspection, then ask them to wrap it around the bottle. As they are doing this, slip your hand into your pocket and pick up a small pile of the broken sweets.

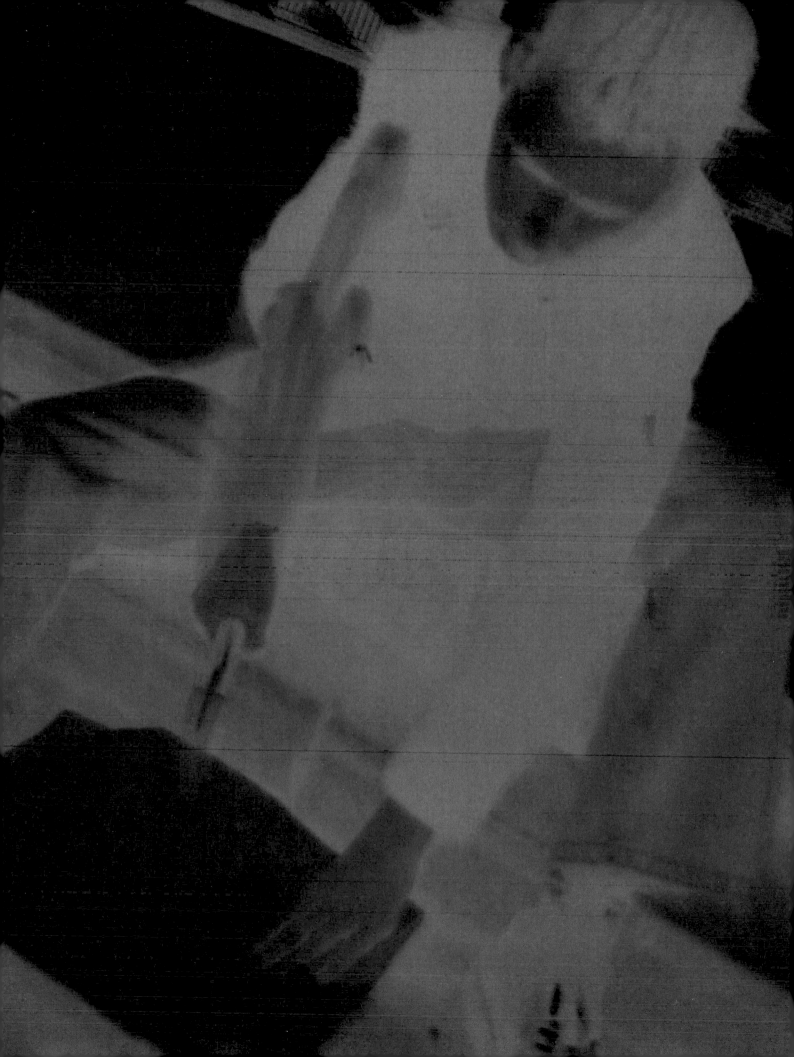

3. When the onlooker has finished wrapping the bottle, take your hammer and - without any warning - hit the bottle. This normally creates a moment of total fear! Continue hitting the bottle, breaking it into lots of little pieces. When you feel that you have broken the bottle up enough, place the hammer down and let everyone know that it is safe to look up!

TIP: *If you really want to freak your spectators out, when you pop the large piece of boiled sweet in your mouth, sneak a blood capsule in there too! That way, when you crunch down on it, your mouth will suddenly be full of blood!*

4. Open up the cloth so that only you can see inside and make a comment, such as, 'Mmm, my favourite.' This will, of course, bemuse your spectators even more. Push the hand holding the crushed sweets into the cloth as though you are going to pick up some shards of glass. With your free hand, lift the cloth up a little more. This will make the glass move and sound as though you are rummaging about in the shards.

*CAUTION: Of course, be very careful that you keep your hands away from the shards!

5. Open out the hand containing the pieces of the sweets, and let go of the cloth with your other hand. Now it is time to use your best acting skills. Place some of the small pieces of 'glass' on your tongue and swallow them - this is guaranteed to freak out your spectators.

Place a larger piece in your mouth, between your back teeth and mime trying to crush the glass. Pausing for dramatic effect, crunch down on the sweets with your teeth. The shock value here is great!

6. All that is left to do is finish off your portion. Don't forget to offer a piece to your spectators - I promise they won't want any! This is a great interlude to any routine that combines regular magic with more screwed up items!
*CAUTION: Finally, make sure you clear up the real glass afterwards it should be easy as it never leaves the cloth!

Eye Popper

TRICK: You are scratching your cheek with a fork, when you unexpectedly sneeze and pierce your eyeball, literally popping it all over yourself! This is truly sick, but with the right crowd, it will go down a storm!

REQUIREMENTS: À fork; a carton of coffee creamer (the sort you can find in fast food restaurants and some coffee shops).

1. Begin by scratching your cheek with the fork. This in itself will be a little disturbing to your audience.

2. With your free hand, take the coffee creamer and hold it between your thumb and index finger. Keep your hand in your lap or resting on the table, so that the creamer is hidden from view.

TIP: This is best performed outdoors – at a picnic for example. As you are eating, keep bringing the fork up and scratching your cheek... make it look like more of an accident!

Eye Popper

3. When you have everyone's attention, screw up your face as if a sneeze is coming. Lift your head up to sneeze and as you bring it back down, ensure the hand holding the creamer comes up and covers one of your eyes.

4. Continue your sneezing motion with your head down and move the fork up to your eye, pushing it into the creamer.

5. If you squeeze as this happens, the cream will explode out of the pot, covering everything in sight! If timed correctly, this looks fantastic.

6. As soon as the creamer has popped, scrunch your eye up and drop your hands to the side. Place the fork down and rub your eye, slowly opening it to show that you are okay. The shots here will give you some idea of the effect this can have, but believe me, it's much more horrifying in the flesh.

The Street Levitation

TRICK: You stand in front of your audience, with your back to them, and float up to 5 inches off the ground!

REQUIREMENTS: This works best with a small group, standing in one place.

1. Ask your audience to stand close together with their arms held out in front of them - to catch you, should you fall backward. Stand 1m in front them and turn away at an almost 45° angle for maximum impact. Reinforce the fact that they must hold out their arms - just in case! This will keep them where you want them.

2. Slowly raise your right foot up on to tip-toe, while leaving your left foot flat and pointing straight out, and keeping both feet together.

TIP: The key to making this illusion work is not to rush. Practise as much as you can - if you can float slowly up and slowly down, the illusion will be perfect!

3. From the perspective of your audience, you appear to be hovering in the air a few inches from the ground. If you want to make it look more dramatic, lift your arms up as you are raising your foot.

It would looks ridiculous from the front, but when viewed from back, off centre, the illusion is very strong and you really will look like you are floating!

The Jacket Levitation

TRICK: You cover your legs with your jacket, leaving your feet sticking out of the bottom. Gracefully, you lift off the ground, floating on the breeze. You sink to the ground, put on your jacket and walk away, feeling as smug as ever.

REQUIREMENTS: A piece of velcro and a jacket.

1. Pull the velcro apart and stick a piece to the inner sides of each of your shoes.

2. Remove your jacket and place it in front of you. Move your feet together, so that the velcro sticks fast, holding your shoes in this position.

TIP: In order to make the jacket levitation look as real as possible, take your time and float as gently as you can.

The Jacket Levitation

3. Carefully remove one of your feet from its shoe and step back slightly.

4. Inch the jacket back, so that your shoes protrude from the bottom. You can now lift both of them up using one foot - the other being used to stabilize you.

4. Viewed from the front this will give the impressive illusion that you are indeed floating behind your jacket.

The Jacket Levitation

5. You can also use the illusion to lean backwards...

6. And float to the side.

6. Once you have 'floated', push your foot back into your shoe. Separate your feet as you brush your jacket away from them (this will also cover the noise of the ripping velcro) and take a bow!

The Floating Can

TRICK: After finishing off the dregs from your can, you make it float between your hands.

REQUIREMENTS: A drink can; a tube of rubber cement.

1. Apply a small amount of rubber cement to the upper portion of the can.

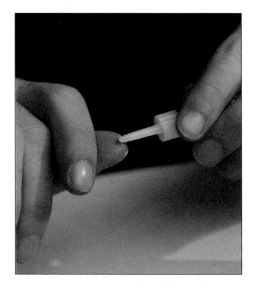

2. Carefully apply some to the end of your thumb. Allow it to dry and you are ready!

3. Drink the contents of the can to make it light, ensuring that your thumb does not touch the glue. Hold the can so that your thumb presses against the glue-covered section of the can and sticks to it.

4. You can now open your hands as wide as possible and the can will remain suspended, apparently floating. By pushing your thumb forwards, the can will appear to have no contact with your hands.

TIP: Only allow the can to 'float' for a few seconds; the longer the can floats without any movement, the more it looks like a trick!

streetsmart

Sometimes when performing, it's good to just step back from the magic and show off! The following are some flourishes that can be used between effects, or even on their own.

The Two-handed Fan

FLOURISH: This is the classic method of fanning playing cards.

1. Start by holding the deck in a dealing grip.

2. With your left hand holding the deck securely, use your right index finger to spread the cards from the top left edge of the deck, which will start to fan the cards.

3. Continue spreading the cards in a semi-circular motion until they make contact with the bottom of your left hand.

TIP: You can also try forming this fan using your thumb to spread the cards, rather than your index finger. This is known as a thumb fan. To close the fan reverse the steps, using your index finger or thumb to sweep the cards together.

The One-handed Fan

FLOURISH: This is the conventional method of fanning a deck with one hand.

1. Pick up the cards with your thumb at one side of the deck and your other four fingers on the other side.

2. Move your index finger and your little finger so that they support the top and bottom of the deck.

3. Remove your thumb so that your fingers alone are supporting the deck.

4. Now place your thumb in contact with the face of the cards and push them upwards. As your thumb does this, use your fingers to pull down from the back, spreading the cards downwards. This will create a fan in your hand. To close the fan, either reverse the whole procedure, squaring the deck as you do so, or use your other hand to square up the cards.

TIP: When you first start to practise the One-handed Fan, you may find it easier to begin with half a deck of cards.

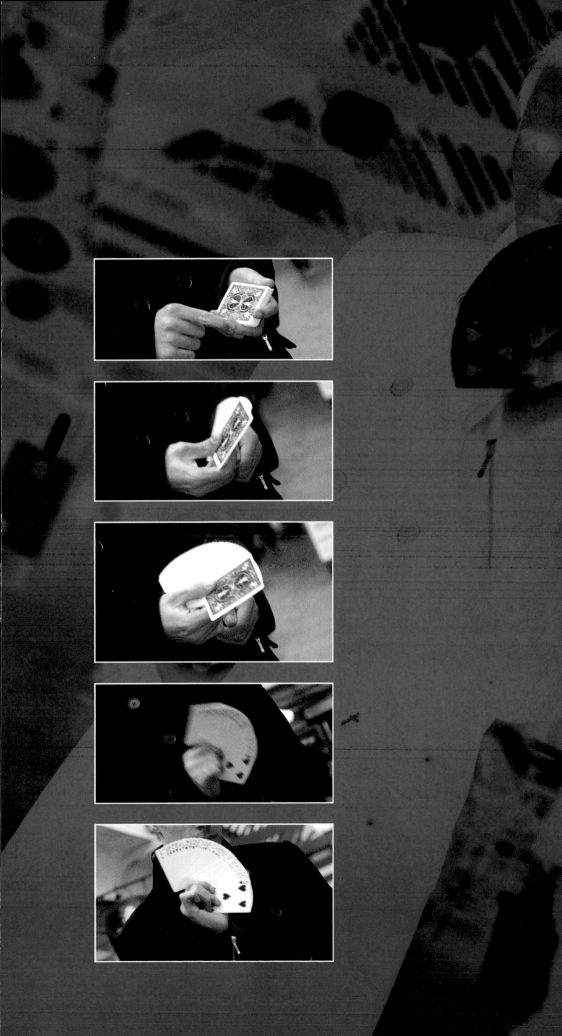

The Double-tiered Fan

FLOURISH: Once you have mastered the One- and Two-handed Fans, this technique will give your audience a visual kick in the teeth.

1. Pick up the cards and cut the deck about halfway down, so that you have two piles that are roughly equal. Take one pile in each hand.

2. Now interweave the cards piles one above the other, so that the cards from each pile alternate one in front of the other with an overlap of a couple of centimetres. This doesn't need to be precise, but the closer you can get it the better it will look.

3. Try to ensure that the very first and last card fall at the same end of the deck, to give you something to hold.

4. Now, carefully perform a One-handed Fan with the lower half of the pack, using either your thumb or your index finger. The upper level of cards will fan with them, creating a visually stimulating display of cards.

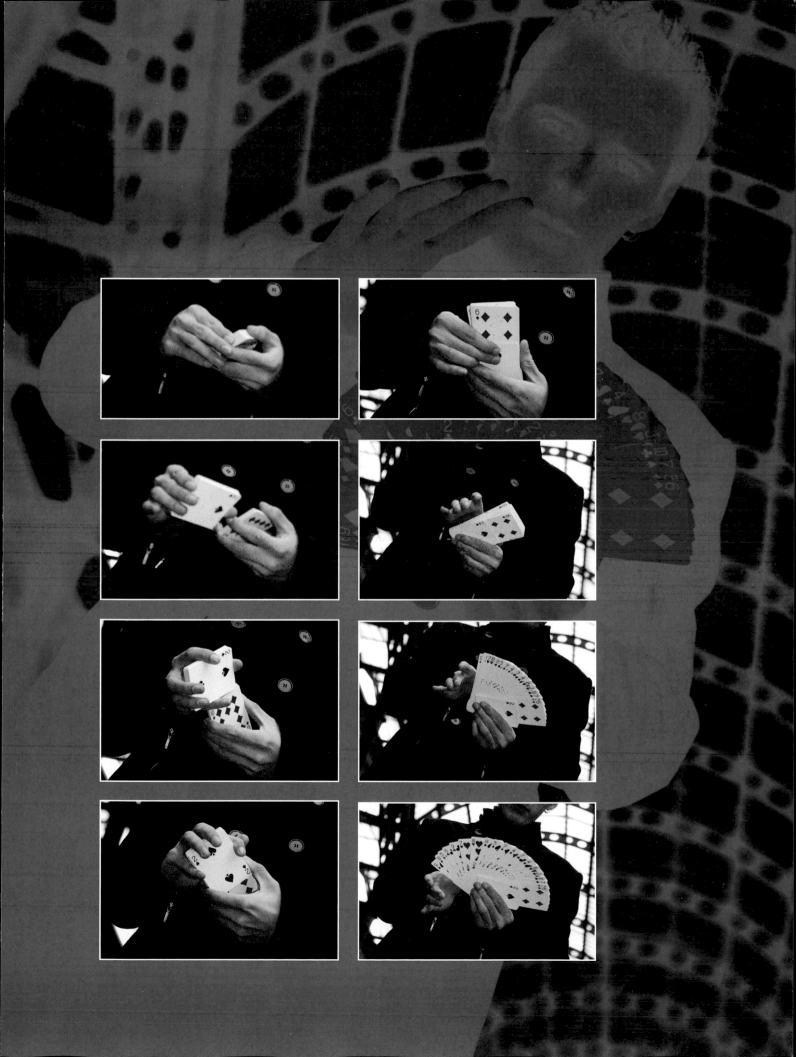

The S-shaped Fan

FLOURISH: The S-shaped Fan is simply a combination of two One-handed Fans that are performed in quick succession.

1. Hold the deck as shown.

2. Bring your free hand up and split the deck at its top edge.

3. Rotate the portion of the deck closest to the left hand so that the cards move into that hand.

TIP: The S-shaped fan looks great performed fast or slow – just try to make the fans as large as possible. It's a pretty display.

The S-shaped Fan

4. Now you are in the position to perform two One-handed Fans. Move the index finger and little fingers of each hand so that they support the top and bottom of the deck. Now press the corresponding thumb of each hand against the face of the cards and push them upwards.

5. As your thumbs do this, use your fingers to pull down from the back, spreading the cards downwards, to create the two fans.

5. Move one fan above the other, so that you create an 'S' shape. This is the final display in the fan sequence.

6. Closing the fan is exactly the reverse, using your index fingers or your thumbs to sweep the cards back together.

The High Flier

FLOURISH: You shoot a playing card out of a deck so that it spins into the air, turns back and lands in your waiting hand... This is a technique that is guaranteed to turn heads. Here's how you do it...

1. Pick up the deck of cards and hold it as if you are about to perform a One-handed Fan (see page 108 for reference).

TIP: *The higher the card flies, the more impressive this will be. With practice, you can really amaze your spectators by shooting a card up into the air, fanning the cards and catching the card in the fan!*

2. Instead of spreading the cards with your thumb, move the top card upwards with a flicking action. This will push the card up and off the deck (see the photo sequence opposite).

3. As the card leaves the deck, it will naturally flick off your index finger, gaining the necessary balance to stabilize in flight. This trick takes time to master, but it is well worth it. You can experiment by using different parts of your thumb to spin the card. With practice, you can send the card flying very high - but watch out, what goes up must come down!

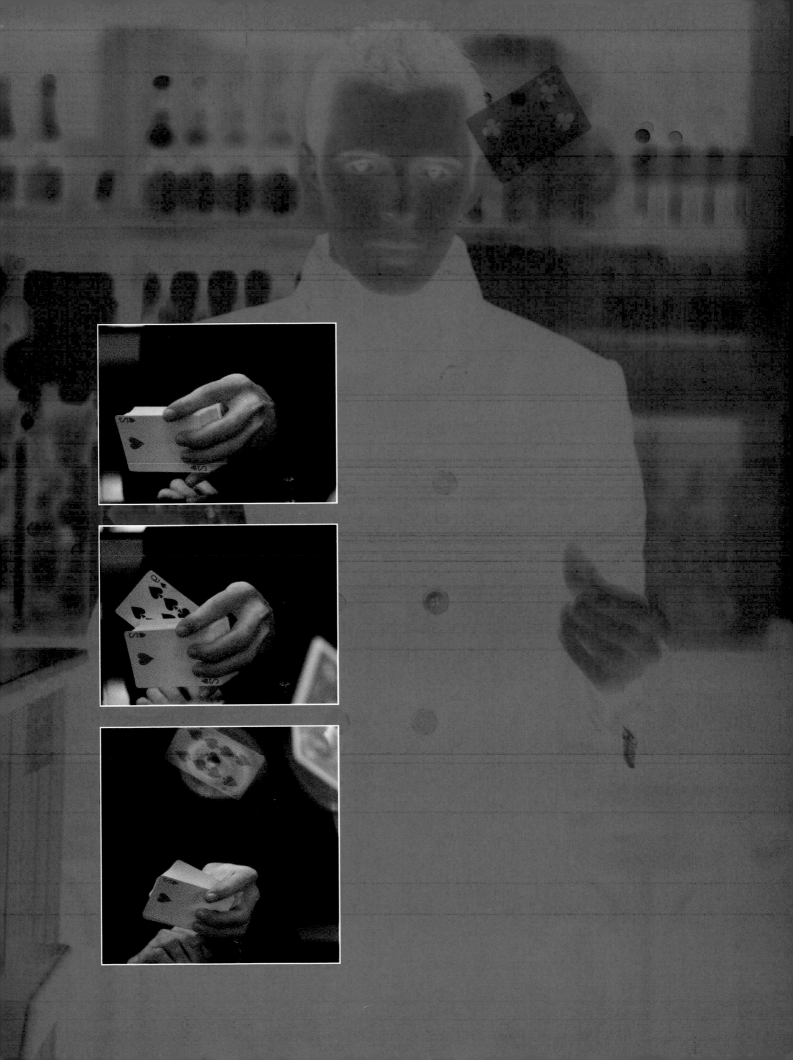

The Gentle Glider

FLOURISH: This is a much more graceful, close-up card flick than the High Flier.

1. Hold the deck as shown, ensuring that your index finger is free.

2. With the tip of your index finger, pull back the top right hand corner of the top card.

3. Release the card with your index finger. It will spin off the deck, flying slightly to the left (or right, if you're left-handed). Practice will teach you how and when to catch it!

TIP: Flicking the card from the deck is only half of the trick. Remember to practise smoothly catching the card in your other hand. Once you have mastered both elements you will be able to glide gently any time!

The One-handed Cut

FLOURISH: This is a really cool way to cut a deck of cards using just one hand.

1. Hold the deck as shown.

2. Release the grip of your thumb very slightly, allowing about half the cards to drop down, still holding them with your fingers.

3. With your index finger, push the lower cards towards your thumb so that they are in a vertical position.

4. The lower cards will then be above the cards in the top half of the deck. The upper cards drop down, allowing the vertical cards to fall on top of them, completing the cut.

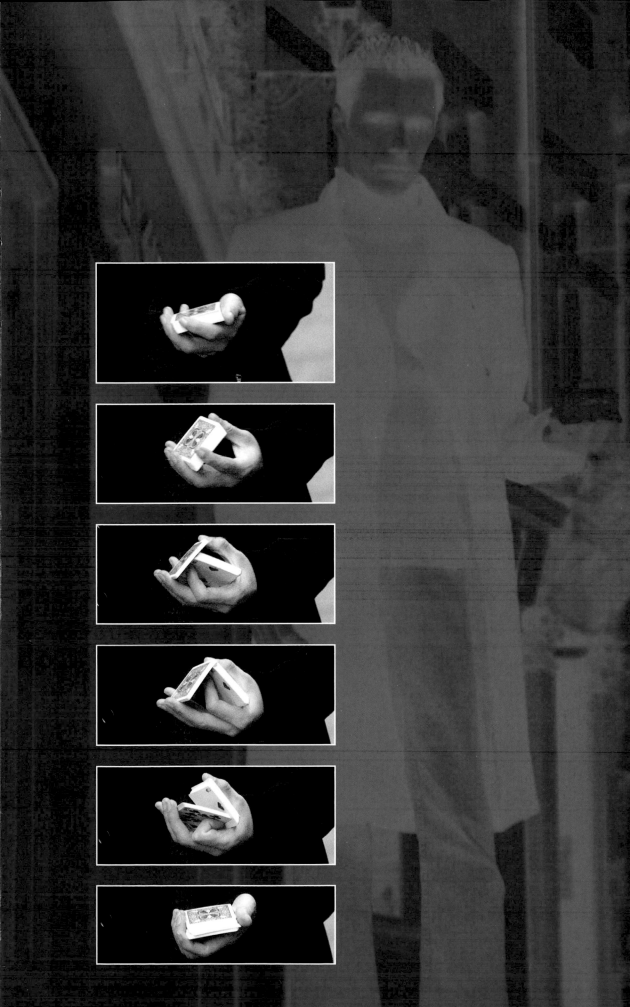

The Coin Roll

FLOURISH: Here is how to roll a coin across your knuckles, just like the gamblers in old Westerns...

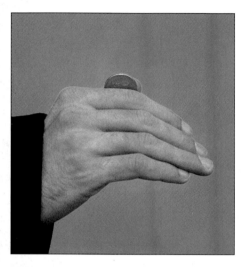

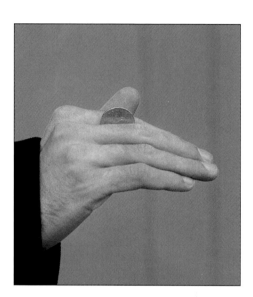

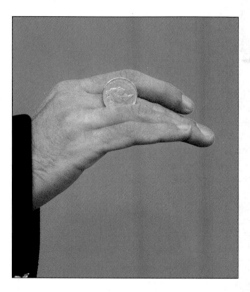

1. Grab a coin - the larger the better. Hold it pinched between your thumb and index finger.

2. Use your thumb to push this coin over the top of your index finger. As the coin rolls over your index finger it will land in the crook between your index and middle finger..

3. You now need to lift your index finger slightly, again rolling the coin, however, this time the coin will roll over your middle finger.

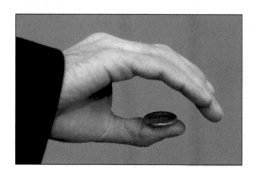

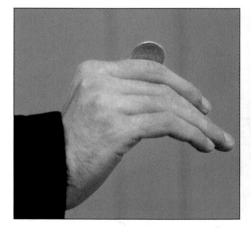

5. As the coin drops between your ring and little fingers, let it slip through the gap between the digits slightly, so that your thumb catches it.

4. Repeat this action to roll the coin over your ring finger.

6. Your thumb then carries the coin back across the palm of the hand, so that another coin roll can begin.

Starting Out and Establishing Yourself

One of the hardest parts of performing magic is actually finding the confidence to go out and do it for real audiences. I've been there myself, and I know as well as anyone how difficult it is to get going. My advice is to be brave! The longer you leave it, the harder it will be.

Start out by performing in front of people you know. The great thing about friends, family or even fellow magicians, is that if you make a mistake, or things aren't as impressive as they could be, they will tell you without making you feel bad about it – it will feel more like constructive criticism. Their advice is the greatest tool available to you. I assure you that once you have performed a few times, you will reach a natural high that really can't be beaten. The buzz that you receive after your first few performances really will make you want to carry on with magic.

However, when you start out, be careful not to take on more than you can handle. This is a common mistake – I've seen plenty of people start off in the magic world and two months into their studies they are accepting paid gigs. Trust me, this won't benefit you in any way. If anything it will hinder your progression.

Some of you, I'm sure, will read this book and keep these tricks in your minds for many years, maybe only performing them once or twice as a hobby. For those of you that do want to progress as serious amateurs, or even develop to performing professionally, your choice of tricks, effects and routines is a very important one.

At the start of any new hobby or occupation, you want to try everything – this is human nature. The same always occurs in magic – within the first six months you will probably spend loads of money buying tricks, books and DVDs, trying to find the latest and greatest magic trick. I won't try to deter you from this, as such curiosity is inevitable, but I will say that sooner or later this will wear off and you will begin to realize that there is a much straighter road to achieving your desired results. Eventually, you will come to accept that not all magic needs to be 'bought', and that basic magic knowledge, along with imagination and personality, are all that you need to start on the road to performing good magic.

Many of the great magicians had certain routines that they would perform over and over again, for which they became renowned. The late, great Albert Goshman, for example, had a beautiful routine that revolved around the simplest of items – sponge balls, a coin and a salt cellar. Despite the simplicity, he had performed it so many times that it reached theatrical perfection, where everything came naturally and there were no 'moves' and no 'funny stuff' – just pure performance.

This kind of simplicity is what you should aim for. If, in your studies, you find something that you really like performing and your spectators enjoy seeing, stick with it. You can use this effect as the basis of your performance and build other tricks around it, forming the whole into a solid, professional performance. The more you get to perform these routines, the better they will be. It goes without saying – practice makes perfect.

When you feel confident enough to take your magic to new audiences, there are bound to be plenty of people that would love to see your magic. You should, however, start small – with complimentary shows. You can visit places such as residential homes, hospitals and charity events, as they will gladly welcome you to perform for them (free of charge, of course). These gigs should be taken and used to their full potential. Not only are they a great opportunity to try out new tricks, but you can also use them to hand out business cards… Most importantly, you get to perform!

Pretty soon, you will get enquiries from people who have seen your act and want you for their events, perhaps even as a paid performer. When this happens it is a good idea to speak to other magicians and determine the going rate for magicians in your area. You don't want to overcharge, but then again you don't want to sell yourself short!

It's always a good idea to make contact with magicians in your region. There are many magic clubs all over the world and a simple search on the Internet should yield plenty of results. You can also contact magic shops as they will advise you of the best place to look for fellow performers. Magic clubs are a great place to socialize with other magicians, who are usually happy to share their ideas and tips with you.

A Few Words On Hecklers

Now, somewhere along the road, you will encounter the magician's nightmare. This is a certain breed of genetically-modified spectators known as 'hecklers'. Hecklers are there purely to make life difficult for you. There is no doubt that you will encounter such audience members in some form – the key is knowing how to deal with them. Think of them as bugs on your window – learn how to wipe them away and carry on along the road!

If you are performing for a group and one person is blatantly not interested, but the rest of the group is, there is no issue. Perhaps this person doesn't enjoy magic, or they are just having a bad day. As long as the rest of the group are enjoying the performance, keep it up! If more than one person has a bored look on their face, either you picked the wrong venue or your performance style needs evaluating – that's for you to decide!

The type of heckler that is the worst kind is the one who won't shut up, co-operate or behave. If a member of your audience is making things difficult for you, the solution is simple. Excuse yourself from the group, table or stage, stating something along the lines of, 'As you don't seem to want to see any tricks today, I'll leave you to enjoy your evening.' As you walk away, rest assured that, if the rest of the group were enjoying the performance, they will turn on the heckler, as he or she has ruined the performance for them. You can probably expect an apology or a request for you to come back a little later on!

Most of the time, heckling can be fun, and it's even beneficial to you. A lot of hecklers do what they do in order to challenge you. Some people want to be centre of attention at all times. If this is the case, great. Let's assume you have a spectator who insists on being the centre of attention – well why not let them! By using them as an assistant and making them the star, you are avoiding all confrontation and there is no issue between you. Sometimes, especially when performing the sort of tricks where the spectators think they know how it works but you prove them wrong, you can even encourage heckling!

It is always a good idea to build up a store of gags and one-liners, as sometimes they can help you really win an audience over! Above all, don't let audience interference panic you at this stage. Most working magicians don't even worry about hecklers, as they have learned over time the best ways to handle them.

Final Thoughts

I hope that you have enjoyed reading this book and I am sure that you will have fun performing these tricks. I hope that at least some of my performance advice will stick with you and help you progress and enjoy magic as much as I do.

Remember that magic is all about one thing and one thing only – entertainment… Make it entertaining and your audience will thank you for it!

Gary Sumpter

Further Reading

Christopher Milbourne, *The Illustrated History of Magic*, Greenwood Press

Karl Fulves, *Self-working Magic* (series), Dover Press

MagicTricks.co.uk, *Everybody's Magic*

Marc Lemezma, *Every Magic Secret Revealed*, New Holland

Marc Lemezma, *Mind Magic*, New Holland

Mark Wilson, *Complete Course in Magic*, Running Press

Martin Gardner, *Mathematics, Magic and Mystery*, Dover Press

Richard Jones, *That's Magic*, New Holland

Magazines

Genii Magazine
Richard Kaufman
4200 Wisconsin Avenue NW
Suite 106–292
Washington, DC 20016
USA
www.geniimagazine.com

Magic Magazine
Stagewrite Publishing, Inc.
6220 Stevenson Way
Las Vegas, NV 89120
USA
www.magicmagazine.com

Magic Week – an online magic newsletter updated weekly
www.magicweek.com

Magic Dealers

Gary Sumpter
Creative Magic
www.gwsmagic.com

MagicTricks.co.uk
Unit 4, Stonestile Business Park
Stonestile Road,
Headcorn,
Kent,
TN27 9PG
www.magictricks.co.uk

Magic Clubs

The Magic Circle
Centre for the Magic Arts
12 Stephenson Way
London NW1 2HD
www.themagiccircle.co.uk

Society of American Magicians
PO Box 510260
St Louis
Missouri 63151–0260
USA

Magic Websites

The Magic Café – an online magic community
www.themagiccafe.com

Index

Acknowledgements

For their kind help with photography, our grateful thanks go out to Browns Restaurant & Bar, Butlers Wharf, Shad Thames, London; The Lockside Lounge, Camden Lock, Camden, London; Fiona Wilson; Gray Lappin; Gülen Shevki-Taylor; Kimberly Allcock-Ainsworth; Lucy Railton; Sophie Stewart; and Stephanie Carey.